HOW TO MAKE
Resin Jewellery

Dedication

For Anna, who finds feathers.

How to Make
Resin Jewellery
With over 50 inspirational step-by-step projects

Sara Naumann

SEARCH PRESS

First published in 2017

Search Press Limited
Wellwood, North Farm Road,
Tunbridge Wells, Kent TN2 3DR

Text copyright © Sara Naumann

Photographs by Paul Bricknell at Search Press Studios

Photographs and design copyright
© Search Press Ltd 2017

ISBN: 978-1-78221-337-6

The Publishers and author can accept no responsibility for any consequences arising from the information, advice or instructions given in this publication.

Readers are permitted to reproduce any of the items in this book for their personal use, or for the purposes of selling for charity, free of charge and without the prior permission of the Publishers. Any use of the items for commercial purposes is not permitted without the prior permission of the Publishers.

Suppliers
If you have difficulty in obtaining any of the materials and equipment mentioned in this book, then please visit the Search Press website for details of suppliers: www.searchpress.com

Printed in China

ACKNOWLEDGEMENTS
I would like to thank the following suppliers:

ICE Resin®: iceresin.com

Ranger Ink: rangerink.com

Nunn Design: nunndesign.com

Yaley Enterprises: yaley.com

Lazertran: lazertran.com

Elizabeth Craft Designs: elizabethcraftdesigns.com

IndigoBlu: indigoblu.com

Plaid: plaidonline.com

Beacon Adhesives: beaconadhesives.com

Hot Off The Press: paperwishes.com

Contents

THE PROJECTS

Introduction

I started making jewellery long ago when I chanced upon some beads in a craft store. An evening of experimentation resulted in a simple bracelet, and I became hooked on the creative and practical possibilities of beading. I was so pleased to create something (no matter how humble) that I could wear to work the next day.

When resin jewellery came to the crafting world, I was intrigued, but also intimidated. These pieces, with their domed surfaces and layers of text and inclusions, were impossibly beautiful. I wondered if I could ever achieve the same results – but I had to try.

I bought a set of ICE Resin® and some bezels and went home to experiment. I was nervous: there's an element of precision required for mixing resin and a limit to the time you have for pouring. I worried that despite my best efforts, my pieces would never look as good as the ones that inspired me. Nevertheless, I went for it.

And it was easy. The measuring was simple. The allotted time was more than enough. The results? Better than I could have hoped for. I was hooked. Again.

Through the years, I've pushed my creative boundaries and tried a lot of different things with resin. Yes, I've made mistakes, I've had air bubbles and overpours and pieces that just didn't end up the way I wanted. Yet those little mistakes are nothing compared to the fun I've had with resin. It's the same feeling I had when I brought home those beads from the craft store so many years ago.

The big reason I love resin? It's a medium that expands to fit your wishes. A simple clear pour over some patterned paper gives you a lovely piece with style and flair. If you want to add inclusions, powders or colouring agents to the mix, suddenly worlds of design options are open to you.

Regardless of your approach, each piece you make will be unique, depending on the resin treatment and the bezels, commercial moulds or surfaces you use. From clean and simple designs to eclectic bohemian styles, resin offers options for lots of different looks and preferences. Whether you want to make yourself a new piece of jewellery, create a gift or make pieces to sell, you can count on resin for a polished, professional result that lasts!

Even better? I think you'll quickly find the fun in resin jewellery – and I believe you'll find yourself just as hooked as I did!

Tools & Materials

Resin jewellery is easy to make in the comfort of your own home and you only need a few tools and materials to get started. Once you have your resin, bezels, some paper and perhaps some colouring agents, you can start to have fun and make unique and beautiful creations.

What is Resin?

Resin epoxy begins with two liquids: one part is resin, the other part is hardener. You mix them using a one-to-one ratio. The liquid will dry, then cure clear and rock-hard.

You can use resin in commercial moulds, as free-form pieces or as a thick, glossy coating to seal elements inside a bezel.

The resin I work with is called ICE Resin®. While there are a few kinds of two-part resin epoxy brands on the market, I've always used ICE Resin® with great success. It cures to a clear, glass-like finish, yet can also be coloured with alcohol inks, paint, powder inclusions and more.

It also has surface tension – imagine a water droplet on a freshly waxed car. That same surface tension allows you to create domed effects. Yet the resin is also self-levelling, and will move to fill every area of a bezel or mould.

The drying time varies between 8–12 hours. I usually do a batch in the afternoon so I can fix any overspills or air bubbles before the piece dries, then allow a complete drying time overnight. You can wear your jewellery as soon as it's dry but take care not to store it in an airtight container until it's cured. Pieces cure in three days.

Whichever brand of resin you use, please be sure to read all the manufacturer's instructions carefully as different brands may vary slightly.

10

Shelf life

Unopened bottles have an indefinite shelf life, but it's best to use the resin within a year of purchasing. Once you open a bottle, air will slowly affect the hardener and cause it to turn yellow. This generally doesn't affect the curing time but will affect the clarity of your finished piece. I still use my yellow-tinted resin, but I add colouring agents to it, rather than use it for a clear pour.

NOTE
UV resin is different from regular resin – it can only be cured with UV rays, such as direct sunlight or a UV lamp, and is not used in this book.

What you need before you pour

There are a few must-have supplies for making resin projects. Because you have a limited 'open time' with the resin mixture, it's a good idea to have all these elements out on your work surface before you start mixing. These items are not listed on the project pages.

Resin epoxy: Several varieties are available, such as EnviroTex Lite® and EasyCast® Clear Casting Epoxy. I like ICE Resin® and that's the brand I've used throughout the book. Other resins will mix in a similar way. Be sure to read the manufacturer's instructions.

Disposable plastic cups: It's very important to measure the two resin parts precisely. Cups with the measurements printed on the side are invaluable.

Disposable stir sticks: Wooden stir sticks – sometimes called craft sticks – are ideal for mixing resin and for drizzling resin into a bezel.

Cocktail sticks: I use these to transfer resin onto small pieces and to guide inclusions into position in the wet resin. They can also be used to pierce any air bubbles you find in the resin (see *Troubleshooting*, page 20).

Drinking straws: Invaluable for eliminating air bubbles; simply blow gently onto the wet resin and the air bubbles will gradually disappear.

Non-stick craft sheet: A non-porous, non-stick craft sheet is essential to protect your work surface. It is coated, so resin paper and free-form shapes peel right off. Drips or spills can be wiped off with a baby wipe. Dried resin is easy to scrape off with a plastic card such as a hotel key card. Alternatively, use a plastic bin bag to protect your table. Be sure to smooth it down and tape it so it stays securely in place. When you're done, it can't be re-used – just throw it away.

Baby wipes: Have them on hand to wipe up any resin spills or overflow.

Flat, level surfaces: I use inexpensive plastic cutting boards (from a well-known Swedish furniture store). One thin cutting board goes underneath my craft sheet. This way I can simply lift the cutting board – and everything on the craft sheet – out of the way.

A smaller, thicker cutting board is also portable. The loop of my bezels can hang over the edge so the bezel lies flat and the resin doesn't overflow.

Foam bases: For post earrings and bangle bracelets, you need a surface into which you can insert the jewellery piece, so it stays upright and level. For rings, I cut niches in a kitchen sponge and insert the rings (see right). Post earrings are poked into a piece of packing foam rescued from recycling. Bangle bracelets are wedged into a niche cut in packing foam.

Gloves and apron: Because you're working with chemicals, you'll want to make sure you protect your skin and clothing. Gloves and an apron are advisable.

ICE RESIN®
JEWELERS GRADE
CRYSTAL CLEAR
part. A Resin 4oz.

ICE RESIN®
JEWELERS GRADE
CRYSTAL CLEAR
part. B Hardener 4oz.

13

Bezels, moulds & more

Resin can be poured into a metal bezel, into commercial moulds or on top of wood pieces – it all depends on the type of jewellery you want to create.

Bezels

Metal bezels are a popular jewellery choice because they're easy to use and give a polished, professional look (see below). Simply drizzle or pour the resin inside. You can add paper or other materials first, or fill with coloured resin.

Several companies produce high-quality metal bezels in a variety of shapes and finishes. A little online research will reveal lots of choice and there are many suppliers with a great range of shapes and finishes ranging from classic to modern. You can choose from sterling silver or plated bezels, depending on your preference. Here I've used plated metal, unless otherwise specified.

Open-back bezels: Some bezels have no back. In this case, you can create one by first placing the bezel onto clear packing tape. Press firmly to create a seal (see above). Pour the resin inside, let it cure and then remove the tape.

Watch-case bezels: You can also use found metal pieces such as old watch casings (see below). A watch case is the flat piece of metal located on the back of a watch. Broken watches are a gold mine for handmade jewellery, and the watch cases can be used as shallow bezels, perfect for unique and dimensional resin pieces. Check thrift stores and online for watch parts that can be used as resin bezels.

Commercial moulds

Reusable plastic moulds are fabulous for creating resin pieces. Look for commercial moulds labelled 'for jewellery casting'. These will allow for easy release of your cured resin piece, which will simply pop right out.

You can also make your own moulds from found items such as ice-cube trays, but for these you will need to coat the inside with a mould release spray before filling them with resin.

Wooden pieces

Wooden shapes can also make great jewellery bases. Scrabble® tiles, game pieces or purchased wooden shapes are ideal and can often be picked up inexpensively.

Craft sheet

Your non-stick craft sheet (see the list of supplies on page 12) isn't just for protecting your work surface – you can also pour resin directly on top, let it cure and then simply peel it off. These so-called 'free-form pieces' are great fun and easy to make; and they can then be filed, punched or simply used as they are.

Papers & inclusions

Your resin jewellery can incorporate lots of different commercial and found elements.

Paper

Paper works beautifully with resin and patterned paper is the quickest, easiest way to get fabulous colour and design into your resin jewellery. Try commercial patterned craft paper, such as scrapbook paper or stationery; handmade paper; origami paper; pages from old or new books; map paper; handwriting; postage stamps; tissue paper; and napkins. You can easily find dozens of designs at your local art and craft supplier or stationers. They're available in different sizes, in colour-coordinating packs or by the sheet.

Raid the recycling bin or charity shop for other options, since you want paper that is lightweight and porous. Older or vintage paper is especially fibrous and will react beautifully to the resin. Slick, glossy or magazine-type paper is coated and generally does not work well.

When choosing patterned papers, consider the size of the printed pattern and the size of your bezel. You can punch single elements from paper with small patterns or portions from a larger design. Use stick glue to glue the paper inside the bezel.

Inclusions

In this book we explore both fine inclusions (those with small granules, such as fine glitter – see below left) and more dimensional inclusions such as found elements (dried flowers and leaves, feathers, buttons and so on – see opposite, bottom). You can easily embed keepsake items or add a dash of sparkle to your jewellery.

Colouring agents

Clear resin can be coloured with a variety of agents, from alcohol ink to paint to nail polish (see right). Simply mix the resin, then add drops of the colouring agent until you have the look you want. Do remember that water and resin won't mix, so water-based media will often not cure properly. Use them sparingly in proportion to the resin.

TIP
You can coat paper with resin to make it translucent, or seal it first to preserve the colours and patterns. See pages 22 and 23 for details.

Resin preparation & mixing

Two-part resin epoxy is available from several manufacturers and for most, the process is the same: simply measure two equal portions of Parts A and B. You can then add colouring agents or inclusions, or use it to coat paper. While resin is a chemical and should be treated carefully, it's easy to mix and use.

Preparing your mixing area

Before you start mixing your resin, it's a good idea to prepare your mixing and curing areas. Have all supplies on hand and the process will be much more efficient. Since you only have about 45 minutes of working time once you mix the resin, you'll want to have everything in place and ready to go.

My curing area is a shelf in a hallway closet where I know the resin will be undisturbed by curious cats and children. I mix my resin at the kitchen table, which is covered with craft sheets, but sports a few dried resin traces nonetheless.

Protect your work surface: Remember that resin is permanent, so protect your table and, if necessary, your floor, with craft sheets and/or plastic bin liners. I place two craft sheets on my table, securing them to the table with masking tape so they don't accidentally slide off with my (wet) resin in tow!

Plan for moving pieces: If you want to transfer resin-filled pieces to another area, place a thin, flat cutting board underneath the craft sheet. This way, you can easily lift the cutting board with the craft sheet on top and transport it to a curing area.

Protect your skin and clothing: Wear an apron, roll up your sleeves and tie back long hair. Wear latex or latex-free gloves to protect your hands, especially if you are coating paper with resin.

Choose the right room: Make sure there's adequate ventilation – although craft resin is generally low-odour, it's still good to have plenty of breathing room. It's best to mix your resin in a warm room.

Have baby wipes on hand: Baby wipes are the best option for cleaning up overspills or wayward drops. Cleaning up with water won't work because resin is not water-soluble.

Be prepared: Any resin left over from your pouring session will need to be discarded – you can't save mixed resin for another time. Have plenty of jewellery pieces or papers on hand – that way you can be sure to use up every drop of your resin mixture without wasting any.

TIP

It is possible to over-stir the resin. Work with a gentle, folding movement rather than a vigorous blending style, which can whip up excess air bubbles.

How to mix resin

1 Mix both resin parts in a mixing cup. Start with Part A resin, then add an equal amount of Part B hardener.

2 Use the stir stick to mix the resin thoroughly. Stir for 2 minutes, until all striations are gone.

3 Let the mixed resin sit for 4 minutes. This allows any air bubbles to dissipate.

4 Hold a drinking straw towards the resin cup and gently blow warm air towards the resin. This will get rid of many of the remaining bubbles.

5 Add resin to your project. From here, you can pour the clear resin into a bezel, coat paper with a sponge dipped in resin or mix the resin with colouring agents, fine inclusions or dimensional inclusions.

19

6 Allow your piece to cure. Place it on a flat, level surface in a dust-free area. Your piece will be dry in about 8–12 hours; the resin will cure in three days. You can work with the piece once it's dry, but don't place it in an airtight container until it's completely cured.

Remember that your batch of resin is good for about 45 minutes, after which time it will begin to set and will need to be discarded. Set a timer if it helps – you'll also notice that the resin will become cloudier and warmer as the clock runs out. All mixing materials and cups should be discarded after use.

Troubleshooting

Working with resin is easy and, like any activity, the more you do, the more comfortable and confident you'll become. Still, you may encounter some bumps along the road. Here, I share my tips on troubleshooting with resin.

Air bubbles

Air bubbles were once my greatest frustration in resin jewellery. It seemed an inevitable part of the process but unfortunately happened all too often on my favourite pieces.

Air bubbles occur when air is introduced to the resin – generally in the pouring and mixing phase. You'll often notice large and small bubbles appear in your bezels immediately after you pour the resin mixture inside. They also occur when dimensional inclusions are placed into the resin in a bezel. Sometimes, bubbles can also form after the resin begins to dry.

What to do?

Here are some cures:

The Drinking Straw Method: If you notice bubbles straight away, simply breathe warm air onto the piece (see below). Blowing gently through a drinking straw is the magic trick. Once I discovered this, my problem with air bubbles virtually disappeared.

After you place your items to cure, check on them every 15 minutes for the next hour. Make sure you have adequate lighting, since bubbles typically form around the edges of a bezel, making them harder to see. Then utilise the Drinking Straw Method and plan to check back in a few minutes.

Cocktail stick and baby wipe: For bubbles that appear after the resin begins to dry, place the piece in strong lighting and have a cocktail stick and baby wipe on hand. Pierce the bubble with the tip of the cocktail stick, working slowly so you don't introduce more air into the resin. If the bubble doesn't pop, wipe the tip of the cocktail stick with the baby wipe and try again.

Disguise: If you discover air bubbles in a piece that has dried or cured, you have two options. If the bubble is near the top of the piece, it can be sanded, then another application of resin added. When sanding resin, be sure to wear a mask and work with adequate ventilation. I confess to not having the greatest success with this method. Instead, I like to add something on top of the air bubble to disguise it, such as a sprinkling of clear fine glitter, a flat inclusion or a word cut from resin-coated paper, then topped with a thin layer of resin.

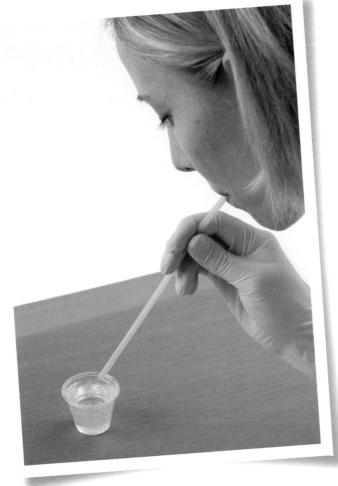

Overpouring

Occasionally, resin might overflow your piece. If you notice straight away, gently lift the piece straight up and use a baby wipe to clean the edges and the bottom, then place it back down. If the resin is in a small area or crevice, wrap the baby wipe around a cocktail stick for better accuracy. If you notice the overflow after the resin is dried but not cured, you can generally chip off the excess resin from the outer edges of a bezel or wooden piece. Sand any rough edges afterwards.

Spills: Use baby wipes to clean up spills immediately. Have a package on hand with the top open so you can easily grab one without fumbling with the package seal!

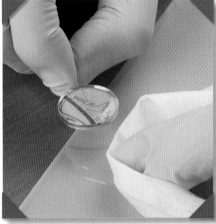
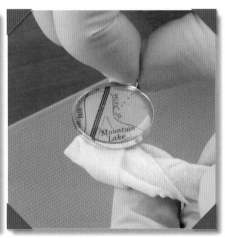

Paper discoloration

Resin will affect paper, soaking into the fibres and tinting them a darker colour (see right). Sometimes this vintage look is what you want; at other times, you may prefer to maintain the original colour. In that case, prevention is the best method. Coat the paper thoroughly with sealer – front, back and all sides – and allow it to dry before you add resin (see page 22).

Sticky resin after curing time

If your resin is still sticky or tacky after 24 hours, something went awry in the measuring or mixing part of the process. Try adding a properly mixed layer of resin on top to remedy this.

TIP

As a teacher, I always encourage my students to embrace any imperfections. Very often, what I consider to be imperfections in my work are actually too small for anyone else to spot! Usually with small pieces such as earrings, no one will notice a tiny bubble along the edge; in that case, it's often better to simply ignore it rather than trying to fix it. At other times, air bubbles actually add to the look of the piece, especially with bohemian-style pieces.

Paper Techniques

Paper is a fabulous material for resin – you can use it as a background in a bezel or cut words or fragments from paper to use as accents. Fibrous papers such as book pages, paper maps and napkins will absorb resin beautifully. Slick, glossy paper (such as magazines) is coated, so it won't have the desired effect.

How to seal paper

When you apply resin directly onto paper, it will tint the paper and darken it. If you'd prefer to maintain the colour and opacity of your paper, seal it before adding resin on top. I like to use Mod Podge® (a sealer, glue and finish in one) to coat my paper – it's inexpensive, easy to find and works like a charm.

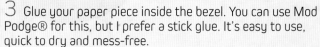

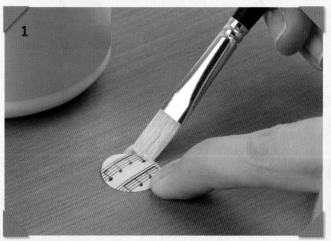

1 Place the paper on your craft sheet. If possible, cut or punch the piece to size.

2 Use a brush or your fingers to apply sealer to the front, back and sides of the paper piece. Place it on the craft sheet and allow to dry. Repeat to ensure all areas of the paper are sealed. Note that if you seal only the front and back, resin can still seep in through the sides of the paper!

3 Glue your paper piece inside the bezel. You can use Mod Podge® for this, but I prefer a stick glue. It's easy to use, quick to dry and mess-free.

Creating a translucent effect

You can also create translucent paper. Coating your paper with resin gives a beautiful, see-through effect. It also allows you to strengthen fragile papers.

To prepare, have a piece of kitchen sponge cut to about 5cm (2in) square. If your sponge has both a spongy side and a scrubbing side, you'll be using the spongy side.

1 Place the paper on your craft sheet. Mix the resin. Dip a corner of a sponge into the resin, then wipe onto the paper. Start in the centre and move out to the edges. Resist the urge to pour the resin onto your paper – it wastes the resin. If you want a thicker coating, let the first layer dry and then apply additional coats as desired.

2 Coat one side of the paper, then flip it over and coat the other side. You won't need as much resin on this side, since it will soak in from the front.

3 Turn the paper face-up. Let it dry for 6–10 hours. Then peel it from the surface of the craft sheet. Use it as is – you can even cut, punch or tear it. You can also create a thicker piece by adding additional layers of resin on top.

NOTE

When coating paper with resin, there's no need to worry about bubbles. You generally don't need to worry about air bubbles when mixing resin with other mediums – either colouring agents or fine inclusions. When I'm making a batch that includes both resin-coated paper and straight-pour pieces, I do the resin paper first. The extra time seems to allow bubbles in the cup to dissipate.

Jewellery findings

Once your resin pieces have dried, you can begin incorporating them into your jewellery. Remember, the resin still needs three days to fully cure. This is where resin jewellery becomes even more personalised – you can incorporate chain, cord or beading techniques into your piece to suit your own style. The fun thing about resin is how versatile the finished pieces can be.

Here's what I've used for my pieces throughout this book:

Chain: I use a lot of metal chain for my pieces. I love the clean, stylish look of chain and how nicely it sets off the resin pieces. And since bezels come in lots of different metal finishes, it's fun to match or contrast the metals.

Chain can be found by the length or on a spool, in a variety of widths and styles. You can cut it with wire cutters and easily add jump rings and clasps. It's a great option for non-beaders or those who are new to jewellery-making.

Ball chain: This is an inexpensive alternative and easy for jewellery beginners. As with chain, it comes on a spool or by the length. You can cut it with scissors and simply slide on a pendant. You'll need a ball chain connector, which clicks on the end of the chain as a closure.

Rattail cord or satin cord: This soft cord is great for those who are sensitive or allergic to metal. You cut the cord with scissors, then slip on the pendant. Add cord ends and close with pliers, then add a clasp.

Jewellery findings: For closing necklaces and bracelets, choose a clasp that works best with your style. I like toggle clasps since they're easy to use and come in a variety of styles.

Jump rings: These are metal rings with an opening. Available in a variety of sizes and finishes, you can use jump rings to attach clasps, bezels or other elements.

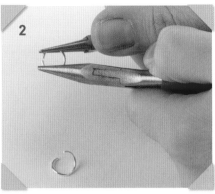

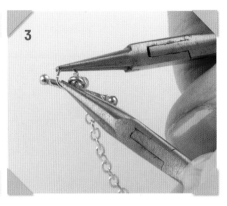

1 Using two pairs of pliers, twist one side of the jump ring towards you and the other side away from you.

2 It's important to twist the piece open rather than pulling it apart, which can weaken the metal and make it impossible to close properly.

3 Once you have attached your clasp or bezel, close the jump ring by simply repeating the process, twisting the two sides together again with the pliers.

Gluing bails: Many bezels have loops, making it easy to attach them to a chain or slip on a cord. Others don't, so you will just need a metal bail and some strong adhesive.

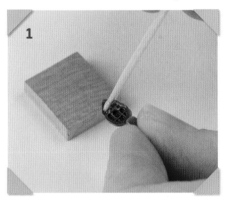

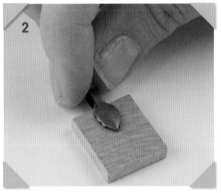

1 Place the jewellery piece face down on your work surface. Use a cocktail stick to apply a small amount of adhesive to the bail.

2 Press the bail gently in place and allow it to dry.

TIP

Be sure to use a strong jewellery glue developed to attach metal to metal or metal to wood. Craft glues are generally not strong enough to last, but there are plenty of suitable ones on the market.

Tools

My most-used jewellery tools are fairly simple. They consist of:

Chain-nose pliers: For opening jump rings and flattening cord ends, these are a great basic.

Wire cutters: For cutting beading wire, chain or ball chain.

Crimping pliers: For creating perfectly round crimps on beaded pieces. However, you will not need these if you plan to work solely with chain or ball chain.

Beads & beading

You can quickly and easily create a beaded necklace or bracelet to set off your piece of resin jewellery.

1 Use a bead board to plan your piece. First, determine how long you want the piece to be, then cut some beading wire about 10cm (4in) longer.

2 Slide a clasp onto the beading wire. Slide on a crimp bead. Pass the end of the beading wire back through the crimp bead. Close the crimp bead with crimping pliers, leaving about 5cm (2in) of loose wire. String a few beads over the doubled wire, then trim the wire.

3 String the remaining beads and bezel. Repeat the process for the other end of the wire and the other half of the clasp.

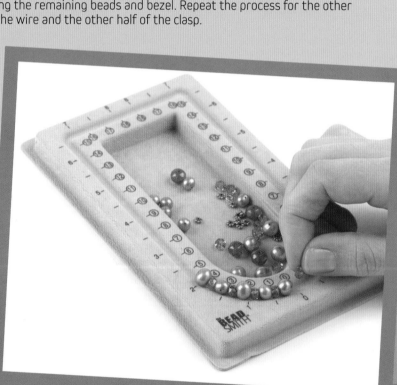

TIP

If you don't have a bead board, simply tape the beading wire to your work table so the beads don't slip off and thread the beads on in the order you wish (see right).

Fitting paper inside a bezel

When working with resin, you'll often want to place paper inside a circular bezel. The easiest way to get a perfect fit is with a craft punch.

Craft punches come in a variety of shapes and sizes. These are invaluable, especially if you plan to do lots of resin pieces. You might not mind hand-cutting one or two paper circles, but preparing for a craft show or a batch of Christmas gifts might change your mind.

The other benefit to punches? By turning them upside down, you can isolate which areas of the paper you want to punch before committing (see below).

If you don't have punches or can't find the right size, a circle template can do the trick, too.

Square and rectangular bezels are a bit easier. You can simply measure the outer parameters of the piece, then measure and cut your paper. You might have to trim down the paper slightly to allow for the width of the bezel edge. For straight lines, use a ruler or paper trimmer. You can also find punches in square and rectangular shapes.

After you have cut or punched your paper, use stick glue or sealer to glue the paper inside the bezel. Apply glue to the entire back of the paper and press it firmly inside the bezel so no resin will seep underneath. Allow it to dry, then add resin.

27

TIPS

› When choosing punches, be sure to compare the *inner* dimensions of the bezel with the size of the punch.

› Craft punches can even cut through resin-coated paper.

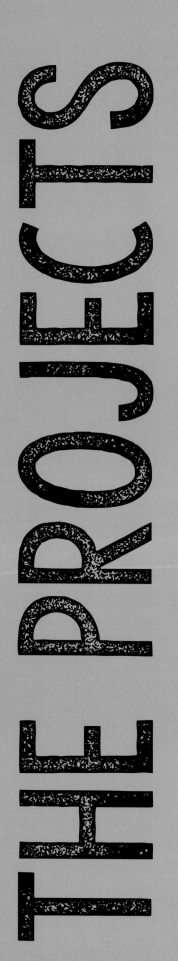

THE PROJECTS

Vintage Map
Necklace 35

Book Lover's
Earrings 36

Sheet Music
Pendant 37

Origami Ponytail
Holder & Ring 38

Floral Necklace
40

Teal Patterned
Earrings 41

Red Speckled
Earrings 46

Magenta Ring 47

Le Voyage Brooch
48

Red Bracelet 49

Flower Pendant
50

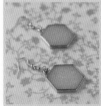

Bird-on-a-Branch
Pendant 51

**COLOURING
AGENTS**

Twilight Glitter
Pendant 58

Glam Pink Glitter
Earrings 59

Wild Plum Heart
Bracelet 60

Hazelnut & Gold
Earrings 61

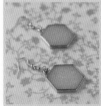

Goldenrod
Earrings 62

Silver & Green
Pearl Necklace 68

Raspberry & Gold
Earrings 69

Perfect Gold
Earrings 70

Winter White
Necklace 71

French Text
Glitter Ring 72

Glitter & Glow
Earrings 73

**3-D
INCLUSIONS**

Mixed Metal &
Pearl Necklace 80

Royal Peacock
Pendant 81

Shine Brooch 82

Dragonfly
Bracelet 83

Feather Pendant
84

Berlin Scrabble®
Tile 91

Forever Blue
Necklace 92

Glitter Square
Necklace 93

Pool Blue Earrings
94

Neon Circle
Necklace 95

Using Paper

SWEET VINTAGE FLORAL EARRINGS

These earrings have a rim around the bezel. A 11mm (⁷⁄₁₆in) punched circle of paper slips under the rim and fits perfectly.

Materials:

- Floral patterned scrapbook paper
- Sealer
- Stick glue
- Round silver 11mm (⁷⁄₁₆in) diameter earrings on ear wires (inner dimensions)

Tools:

- 11mm (½in) circle punch
- Packing foam
- Paintbrush

1 Punch two circles of patterned paper. Coat with sealer, allow to dry and glue one inside each bezel.

2 Insert the earrings into a foam base. Make sure the bezels are level.

3 Mix the resin, pour into the bezels and allow to cure.

HANDMADE PAPER CUFF BRACELET

This cool leather cuff bracelet makes a bold fashion statement, especially with a personalised bezel accent. The handmade paper was actually gift wrap on a birthday present – it was just too pretty not to use! Because the paper is thick and fibrous, I coated it twice with sealer before adding resin.

Materials:

- Orange patterned handmade paper
- Sealer
- Stick glue
- Faux-antique gold ornate 3cm (1¼in) diameter screw-back bezel (inner dimensions)
- 3cm (1¼in) wide brown leather cuff bracelet

Tools:

- 3cm (1¼in) circle punch
- Packing foam
- 1.8mm (¹⁄₁₆in) metal hole-punch pliers
- Chain-nose pliers
- Flush cutters
- Nail file

1 Punch a circle of handmade paper. Coat with sealer, then allow to dry and repeat. Glue the circle inside the bezel.

2 Insert the bezel into a foam base. Mix the resin, pour into the bezel and allow to cure.

3 Use the hole punch pliers to punch a hole in the centre of the leather cuff. Insert the screw shank through the cuff and tightly screw on the nut with chain-nose pliers.

4 Use the flush cutters to cut off excess screw shank. Place the flush cutters at the base of the screw, turn the cuff upside down and cut – otherwise the excess shank can go flying.

5 Use the file to sand the edges of the shank to make it smooth.

TRAVELLER'S CUFFLINKS

A great gift idea for the guy who loves adventure and travel, or a special way to remember a holiday journey or honeymoon travel!

Materials:

➤ Map paper
➤ Sealer
➤ Stick glue
➤ Sterling silver plated 2.1cm (¾in) square cufflinks, (outer dimensions), 5mm (⅛in) in depth

Tools:

➤ 1.5cm (⅝in) square punch
➤ Packing foam

1 Punch two pieces of map paper. Coat with sealer and allow to dry. Glue the paper shapes inside each cufflink bezel.

2 Tuck in the cufflink shanks, then insert the cufflinks into a foam base.

3 Mix the resin, pour into the bezels and allow to cure.

Alternative project

Before you glue the paper inside this Streets of San Francisco ring, slip it on your finger to make sure you position the text or pattern reading the way you want.

VINTAGE MAP NECKLACE

The petite size of this bezel makes it ideal for a short or choker-style necklace.

Materials:

- Map paper
- Sealer
- Stick glue
- Antique-style round silver 1.5cm (⅝in) diameter pendant bezel with loop, 3mm (⅛in) in depth (inner dimensions)
- 4 7mm (¼in) silver jump rings
- 36cm (14in) of silver chain
- Antique-style silver 12mm (½in) toggle clasp

Tools:

- 1.5cm (⅝in) circle punch
- Chain-nose pliers

1 Punch a circle of map paper. Coat with sealer and allow to dry. Glue the circle of paper inside the bezel.

2 Place the bezel on a raised, flat surface with the loop hanging over the edge. Mix the resin, pour into the bezel and allow to cure.

3 Use the pliers to open one jump ring. Slip on one end of the chain and one half of the clasp. Repeat to add the second half of the clasp to the other end of the chain.

4 Use the pliers to open a third jump ring. Slip on the cured pendant and the fourth jump ring. Close the third jump ring. Open the fourth jump ring and attach to the centre of the chain.

BOOK LOVER'S EARRINGS

Dictionary paper is great for resin jewellery – the font is usually quite small, so it fits perfectly inside smaller bezels.

Materials:

- French dictionary paper
- Sealer
- Stick glue
- Round antique copper 1.3cm (½in) diameter pendant with ornate bezel and single loop, (inner dimensions)
- 2 ear wires with copper ball

Tools:

- 1.3cm (½in) circle punch
- Chain-nose pliers

1 Punch two circles of text paper. Coat with sealer, then allow to dry and glue inside each bezel.

2 Place the bezels on a flat surface. Mix the resin, then pour into each bezel. Allow to cure.

3 Use the pliers to open the bottom loop of the ear wire. Slip on the cured bezel. Close the loop. Repeat for the second earring.

SHEET MUSIC PENDANT

This pendant is made in two stages; the first is to coat the sheet music paper with resin to make it translucent and the second is to 'dome' the bezel.

Materials:
- Sheet music
- Stick glue
- Jewellery glue
- Round silver 3cm (1¼in) diameter bezel with loop (inner dimensions)
- Approx. 56cm (22in) of black rattail cord
- 2 silver cord ends
- 2 medium (5mm/³⁄₁₆in) silver jump rings
- Silver toggle clasp
- 1 large (6mm/¼in) silver jump ring

Tools:
- Sponge
- 3cm (1¼in) circle punch
- Chain-nose pliers

1 Use the sponge to coat a piece of sheet music with resin. Allow to cure.

2 Punch a circle of translucent sheet music and glue inside the bezel. Allow to dry.

3 Place the bezel on a flat surface. Mix the resin, then pour into the bezel. Allow to cure.

4 Use jewellery glue to glue each end of the rattail cord into a cord end. Allow to dry, then use the tip of the pliers to gently fold in each side of the cord end.

5 Use the pliers to open one medium jump ring. Slip on the circular half of the toggle clasp and one of the cord ends. Repeat with the bar half of the clasp and the other end of the cord.

6 Use the pliers to open the large jump ring. Slip on the pendant and the cord. Close the jump ring.

ORIGAMI PONYTAIL HOLDER & RING

For hair accessories that will take a lot of handling, be sure to use a metal-to-metal glue to secure the ponytail holder to the back of the bezel.

Materials:

- Origami paper
- Sealer
- Stick glue
- Large round brass 3.5cm (1⅜in) diameter bezel (inner dimensions)
- Elastic ponytail holder
- Silver bracket-style ponytail holder
- Jewellery glue

Tools:

- 3.5cm (1⅜in) circle punch

1 Punch a circle of origami paper. Coat with sealer, then allow to dry and glue inside the bezel.

2 Mix the resin, then pour into the bezel. Allow to cure.

3 Nest an elastic ponytail holder into the groove of the silver ponytail holder, then glue the metal piece to the back of the bezel. Allow to dry.

This gorgeous silver ring bezel is one of my favourites – the square shape pairs perfectly with the curved lines of the flower origami paper to create visual balance.

Materials:

- Origami paper
- Sealer
- Stick glue
- Adjustable silver 1.6cm (⅝in) square ring, 3mm (⅛in) depth (inner dimensions)

Tools:

- 1.5cm (⅝in) square punch
- Packing foam

1 Punch a square of origami paper. Coat with sealer, then allow to dry and glue inside the bezel.

2 Insert the ring into a foam base. Mix the resin, pour into the bezel and allow to cure.

FLORAL NECKLACE

When working with napkins or tissues, first separate the plys to use only the top patterned one. A punch won't cut through the soft fibres of the napkin, so it's best to stiffen it first with resin, which will also make the design translucent. Simply glue the punched or cut piece into a bezel, or layer it on another paper for dimension. Add a second application of resin on top.

Materials:

- Floral napkin
- Sealer
- Stick glue
- Round silver 3cm (1¼in) bezel with ornate edge (inner dimensions)
- 3 4mm (⅛in) silver jump rings
- Silver toggle clasp
- Approx. 38cm (15in) of silver chain

Tools:

- Kitchen sponge
- 3cm (1¼in) circle punch or circle template
- Chain-nose pliers

1 Place the napkin on the craft sheet. Mix the resin, then use the sponge to apply resin to the napkin, coating the back and front. Allow to cure.

2 Peel the napkin off the craft sheet and use the circle punch or stencil to create a circle. Glue the circle into the bezel.

3 Place the bezel on a flat surface. Mix the resin and pour into the bezel. Allow to cure.

4 Use the pliers to open a jump ring and slip on the circular half of the toggle clasp and one end of the chain. Close the jump ring. Repeat to attach the bar half of the toggle clasp to the other end of the chain.

5 Find the centre of the chain. Use the pliers to open the third jump ring. Slip on the pendant and the centre link on the chain. Close the jump ring.

TEAL PATTERNED EARRINGS

Since this napkin had a lot of white in the design, I backed the resin-coated circles with white cardstock so the teal pattern shows up. A sprinkling of clear fine glitter adds a touch of sparkle.

Materials:

- Patterned napkin
- White cardstock
- Sealer
- Stick glue
- 2 round silver 1.2cm (½in) diameter post earrings (inner dimensions)
- 2 earring backs
- Clear fine glitter

Tools:

- 1.2cm (½in) circle punch
- Kitchen sponge
- Packing foam

1 Place the single ply of the napkin on a craft sheet. Mix the resin, then use the sponge to apply resin to the napkin, coating the back and front. Allow to cure.

2 Peel the napkin off the craft sheet and punch two circles.

3 Punch two circles of white cardstock. Coat with sealer and allow to dry. Glue a napkin circle on top of each cardstock circle. When dry, glue each layered piece into a bezel.

4 Insert the earrings into a foam base. Mix the resin, then pour into the bezels. Sprinkle with clear fine glitter. Allow to cure, then add the earring backs.

Alternative project

Have a look in your local newsagent or pharmacy and you'll find lots of novelty patterned tissue packs. I thought these birdies were adorable, and just the right size to fit inside a bezel.

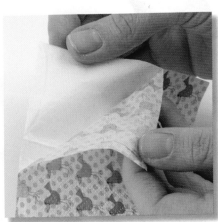

Separating the plys of tissue paper.

CLASSIC BLACK HAIRPIN

Decorative washi tape comes in lots of different colours and designs. The patterns are small, making them the perfect size for jewellery. Adhere the low-tack tape onto paper, then punch and glue.

Materials:

- Black herringbone washi tape
- White cardstock
- Sheet music
- Stick glue
- Sealer
- Round wooden game piece
- Silver bobby pin, 1cm (³⁄₈in) diameter round pad
- Jewellery glue

Tools:

- 2cm (¾in) circle punch
- Cocktail stick

Attaching washi tape and sheet music to cardstock.

1 Place a strip of washi tape onto white cardstock. Glue a strip of sheet music parallel to it, leaving a small space (approximately 1mm/¹⁄₁₆in) between the two.

2 Punch a circle from the washi tape piece. Coat with sealer and allow to dry, then glue to the flat side of the round wooden game piece. Allow to dry, then place on a flat surface.

3 Mix the resin, then pour onto the game piece. Use the cocktail stick to gently guide the resin to the edges. Allow to cure.

4 Glue the game piece to the flat pad of the pin using jewellery glue.

STRIPES & DOTS EARRINGS

I like to combine a patterned washi tape with a solid-coloured tape – this gives a nice visual balance as the stamped bubble wrap will show up more vividly on the solid tape.

Materials:

- Solid blue and orange/blue striped washi tape
- White cardstock
- Yellow acrylic paint
- Sealer
- Stick glue
- Round gold 2cm (¾in) diameter earrings (inner dimensions)

Tools:

- Approx. 6cm (2⅜in) of bubble wrap
- Sponge or foam brush
- 2cm (¾in) circle punch
- Packing foam

1 Place a strip of blue washi tape onto white cardstock. Place a strip of striped washi tape parallel to it, leaving a small space (approximately 1mm/¹⁄₁₆in) between the two.

2 Use the sponge or foam brush to apply yellow paint to the textured side of the bubble wrap. Turn it over and stamp the paint onto the washi tape cardstock piece. Allow to dry.

3 Punch two circles. Coat with sealer and allow to dry. Glue one inside each earring.

4 Insert the earrings into a foam base. Mix the resin, pour into the bezels and allow to cure.

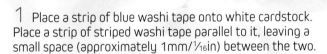

Alternative project

A thick ball chain works perfectly for this bold Copper Collage Pendant, which can be worn short or long. Ball chain is easily cut with scissors so you can achieve the perfect length.

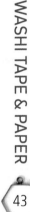

VINTAGE ROSES CHARM

Stamped images are great fun for resin jewellery. You can simply stamp an image, or colour it with pencils or markers. Look for small stamps that fit inside a bezel, or punch sections from a larger stamped image.

Simply tap the stamp onto an inkpad to ink it completely. Turn the inked stamp over and press onto your paper, then lift straight up. Don't rock the stamp as you press. Clean the stamp with a baby wipe and let the stamped image dry. For resin work, it's best to use a dye-based inkpad to stamp your image. Coat the image with sealer before adding it to your bezel, to make sure the ink doesn't bleed or smear.

Materials:

- ➤ White acrylic paint
- ➤ Book paper
- ➤ Sealer
- ➤ Stick glue
- ➤ 3cm (1¼in) diameter watch case (inner dimensions)
- ➤ 3.8cm (1½in) diameter silver badge clip
- ➤ 8mm (5/16in) silver jump ring
- ➤ Silver bail
- ➤ Jewellery glue

Tools:

- ➤ 3cm (1¼in) circle punch
- ➤ Chain-nose pliers
- ➤ Paintbrush
- ➤ Rose border stamp
- ➤ Acrylic stamping block
- ➤ Black dye-based inkpad
- ➤ Green and red fine-tip markers
- ➤ Clear packing tape

1 Paint a piece of book paper, allowing some words to faintly show through. Allow to dry.

2 Stamp the rose border stamp on the painted book paper. Let the ink dry. Use the markers to colour in the rose and leaves. Punch into a circle, then coat with sealer. Let it dry and glue inside the watch case.

3 Wrap clear packing tape around the outside edge of the watch case to block any open areas where the resin could seep out. Place the watch case on a flat surface. Mix the resin, then pour into the watch case bezel. Allow to cure.

4 Remove the packing tape. Glue the bail to the back of the watch case using jewellery glue. Use the pliers to open a jump ring. Slip on the cured bezel and the loop of the badge clip. Close the loop.

STAMPED BICYCLE PENDANT

The scalloped edge of the bezel adds charm to a simply stamped image.

Materials:

- Green patterned paper
- Sealer
- Stick glue
- Ornate round silver cm (1¼in) diameter bezel with loop (inner dimensions)
- 5mm (³⁄₁₆in) silver jump ring
- 40cm (15¾in) of 1mm (¹⁄₁₆in) silver ball chain plus connector

Tools:

- Bicycle stamp
- Acrylic block
- Black dye-based inkpad
- 3cm (1¼in) circle punch or circle template
- Chain-nose pliers

1 Stamp the bicycle on the green paper. Punch or cut into a circle. Coat with sealer. Allow to dry, then glue inside the bezel.

2 Place the bezel on a flat surface. Mix the resin, then pour into the bezel. Allow to cure.

3 Use the pliers to open the jump ring. Slip the jump ring onto the pendant. Close the jump ring. Add the connector to one end of the ball chain. Slip on the pendant.

Alternative project

I wanted these Teal & Copper Letter Earrings to match, so I stamped the alphabet twice and punched circles from the same section. You could punch twice from the same stamped image to get coordinating earrings that don't match exactly – the choice is yours!

Stamping onto paper.

RED SPECKLED EARRINGS

Heat embossing is a great way to add texture and colour. It's easy to create an abstract background with embossing ink, powder and a brayer (hand roller). See below for the technique.

Materials:

- ❯ Red embossing powder
- ❯ Book paper
- ❯ Stick glue
- ❯ Clear embossing ink
- ❯ Small round 1.2cm (½in) diameter earrings (inner dimensions), 2.5mm (⅛in) in depth

Tools:

- ❯ Brayer
- ❯ Heat tool
- ❯ 1.2cm (½in) circle punch
- ❯ Packing foam

1 Brayer and emboss with red powder on the margin of the book paper. Punch two circles. Glue one into each bezel, slipping the paper underneath the rim of the bezel.

2 Insert the earrings into a foam base. Mix the resin, pour into the bezels and allow to cure.

Heat embossing

1 Roll the brayer through the clear embossing inkpad. Roll it onto the paper or cardstock.

2 Immediately sprinkle with embossing powder. Tap off excess powder and return it to the jar.

3 Use the heat tool to melt the embossing powder on the paper. It's melted when it becomes shiny. Then cut or punch before sealing and placing inside your bezel.

MAGENTA RING

Here I brayered the embossing ink quite heavily, so there's very little of the white cardstock showing – just enough to provide some contrast but not enough to require sealing before adding resin.

Materials:
- Magenta embossing powder
- White cardstock
- Round adjustable 1.8cm (¾in) diameter silver ring (inner dimensions), 2mm (¹⁄₁₆in) in depth
- Stick glue
- Clear embossing ink

Tools:
- Brayer
- Heat tool
- 2cm (¾in) circle punch
- Packing foam

1 Brayer and emboss with magenta powder on white cardstock (see opposite). Punch a circle. Glue it inside the ring bezel and allow to dry.

2 Insert the ring into a foam base. Mix the resin, pour into the bezel and allow to cure.

Alternative project
For this Sunshine Yellow Ring design (above), I used painted book paper and brayered lightly with the embossing ink so more of the paper shows through the embossing powder.

LE VOYAGE BROOCH

Creating this bezel in two pour sessions means I have extra space and depth between the inked background and the words. When you add your words, don't forget – to make this a brooch, you need to position the bezel loop at the bottom!

Materials:

> Teal dye-based inkpad
> White cardstock
> Sealer
> Stick glue
> 2cm (¾in) round silver pendant with loop (inner dimensions)
> Computer-generated word or word cut from text paper
> 2 8mm (¼in) silver jump rings
> Silver Eiffel Tower charm
> Silver pin back
> Jewellery glue

Tools:

> 2.2cm (⅞in) circle punch
> Cocktail stick
> Chain-nose pliers

1 Press the inkpad lightly onto the white cardstock. Punch a circle, then coat with sealer and allow to dry.

2 Glue the punched cardstock into the bezel. Place the bezel on a raised, flat surface with the loop hanging over the edge.

3 Mix the resin and pour into the bezel, but only to the rim of the bezel, so you don't create a dome. Allow to cure.

4 Coat the words with sealer and allow to dry. Use sealer to glue them onto the cured resin bezel. Place the bezel on a raised, flat surface with the loop hanging over the edge. Use the cocktail stick to apply resin to the top of the cured bezel, guiding the resin to the edges of the bezel to create a domed effect. Allow to cure.

5 Use the pliers to open one jump ring. Slip on the Eiffel Tower charm. Close the jump ring. Open the second jump ring and slip on the first jump ring and the loop of the bezel. Close the jump ring.

6 Glue the pin back to the back of the bezel using jewellery glue.

RED BRACELET

Clean and simple, this cheerful red pendant adds movement to a chain bracelet. Opt for chunky chain, as I have here, or choose a more delicate chain for a completely different look.

Materials:

- Red dye-based inkpad
- White cardstock
- Sealer
- Stick glue
- Round silver 2cm (1¾in) diameter pendant with loop (inner dimensions)
- 6mm (¼in) medium silver jump ring
- 16cm (6¼in) of silver chain
- Silver lobster claw clasp
- 8mm (⁵⁄₁₆in) large silver jump ring

Tools:

- 2cm (¾in) circle punch
- Chain-nose pliers

1 Press the inkpad lightly onto the white cardstock. Punch a circle, then coat with sealer and allow to dry.

2 Glue the punched cardstock into the bezel. Place the bezel on a raised, flat surface with the loop hanging over the edge.

3 Mix the resin, pour into the bezel. Allow to cure.

4 Use the pliers to open one medium jump ring. Slip it on one end of the chain. Close the jump ring.

5 Open the second medium jump ring. Slip on the clasp and the other end of the chain. Close the jump ring.

6 Find the centre of the bracelet chain. Use the pliers to open the large jump ring. Slip on the pendant and the centre link of the bracelet chain. Close the jump ring.

Alternative project

For these Petite Purple Earrings, I glued lightly inked cardstock onto the flat pad of a post earring, then added resin on top.

FLOWER PENDANT

This is a fabulous technique. You can print photographs onto waterslide decal paper (a type of image transfer paper) using your home printer. I used Lazertran paper. The great fun comes in printing photos onto this transparent film, then layering the image on top of book paper, sheet music or patterned paper – the Lazertran will mute the pattern underneath, giving you fabulous dimension. And because waterslide decal paper is non-porous, you won't need to coat it with sealer before adding resin.

Materials:
- Waterslide decal paper
- Sealer
- Book paper
- Large silver 3 x 2cm (1¼ x ¾in) rectangle pendant with loop (inner dimensions)
- Stick glue
- 6cm (2⅜in) of 3mm (⅛in) silver ball chain plus connector

Tools:
- Shallow pan of water
- Kitchen paper

1 Print a photo on waterslide decal paper, then soak in a shallow pan of water and separate the image from the backing paper. Pat dry with kitchen paper. Use sealer to adhere it to a piece of text paper. Allow to dry, then cut a rectangle to fit inside the bezel. Glue the photo into the bezel. Allow to dry.

2 Mix the resin. Place the bezel on a raised, flat surface with the loop hanging over the edge. Pour the resin into the bezel and allow to cure.

3 Add the connector to one end of the ball chain. Slip on the pendant.

Alternative project
You'll start to look at your photos differently as you develop an eye for which portions can fit into a bezel – even the tiniest areas of a photo can be used for jewellery, as shown in these Orange Post Earrings.

BIRD-ON-A-BRANCH PENDANT

A large bezel such as this one is perfect for a bigger image. I photographed this pretty bird one cold winter's day. To keep the look spare and simple, I first painted the book paper before layering with the image – this knocks back the contrasting text and creates a soft background. Small silver stickers add a touch of shine.

Materials:

- Book paper
- White paint
- Waterslide decal paper
- Sealer
- Stick glue
- Silver 3.5cm (1⅜in) diameter pendant with knob and loop (inner dimensions)
- Small metallic silver circle stickers
- Jewellery glue
- 56cm (22in) of black rattail cord
- 2 silver cord ends
- Silver spring ring clasp
- Silver textured 5mm (³⁄₁₆in) jump ring

Tools:

- Paintbrush
- Shallow pan of water
- Kitchen paper
- 3.5cm (1⅜in) circle punch
- Chain-nose pliers

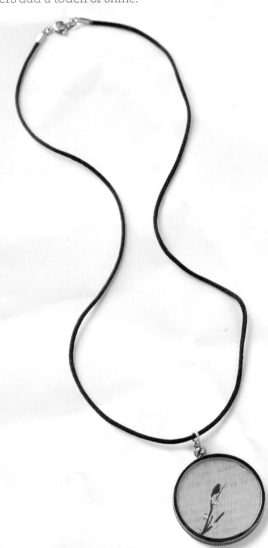

1 Paint some book paper white, leaving the text slightly legible.

2 Print a photo on waterslide decal paper, then soak and separate the image from the backing paper. Use sealer to adhere it to the text paper. Allow to dry, then punch a circle. Glue the circle into the bezel. Add three small metallic silver circle stickers to the photo.

3 Mix the resin. Place the bezel on a raised, flat surface with the loop hanging over the edge. Pour the resin into the bezel and allow to cure.

4 Using jewellery glue, stick each end of the rattail cord into a cord end. Allow to dry, then use the tip of the pliers to gently fold in each side of the cord end.

5 Use the pliers to open the small jump ring on one end of the spring ring clasp. Slip on one of the cord ends. Close the jump ring. Repeat with the other half of the clasp and the other end of the cord.

6 Use the pliers to open the textured jump ring. Slip on the pendant, then slip on the rattail cord. Close the jump ring.

SWIRLY CURVES BROOCH

Lightweight, metallic and iridescent sheets of mylar can be punched or cut with scissors, and embossed with embossing folders for added dimension. Sand the surface of the embossed design to reveal the white inner core of the mylar sheet. Because they're a non-porous material, there's no need to coat them with a sealer— simply glue them right into your bezel and add resin. I used a brand called Shimmer Sheetz.

Materials:

- Light blue mylar sheet
- Stick glue
- Round silver 3cm (1¼in) diameter brooch with ornate border (inner dimensions)

Tools:

- Embossing folder (Swirly Curves)
- Embossing machine
- Sandpaper
- Safety mask
- 3cm (1¼in) circle punch
- Tissue
- Packing foam

1 Emboss and sand the mylar sheet. Use a tissue to brush off the residue. Punch a circle and glue it inside the brooch.

2 Insert the brooch into a foam base. Mix the resin, then pour it into the bezel. Allow to cure.

TIP

When sanding the mylar sheets, be sure to wear a mask and work with adequate ventilation.

LEAF BRANCHES PENDANT

A large embossing plate pattern such as this Leaf Branches design gives you plenty of area from which to choose your design. Hold the punch upside down so you can see exactly which portion you want to capture before you punch.

Materials:

- Orange mylar sheet
- Stick glue
- Round silver 3cm (1¼in) diameter bezel with loop (inner dimensions)
- 3 medium silver 5mm (¼in) jump rings
- Silver toggle clasp
- Approx. 45cm (17¾in) of silver chain

Tools:

- Embossing folder (Leaf Branches)
- Embossing machine
- Sandpaper
- Safety mask
- 3cm (1¼in) circle punch
- Tissue
- Chain-nose pliers

1 Emboss and sand the mylar sheet. Use a tissue to brush off the residue. Punch a circle and glue it inside the bezel.

2 Place the bezel on a raised, flat surface with the loop hanging over the edge. Mix the resin, then pour into the bezel and allow to cure.

3 Use the pliers to open one jump ring. Slip on the circular half of the toggle clasp and one end of the chain. Close the jump ring. Repeat for the second jump ring and the bar half of the clasp.

4 Find the centre of the chain. Use the pliers to open the third jump ring and slip on the pendant and the centre loop of the chain. Close the jump ring.

Alternative project

You don't always have to sand the mylar sheet. For these Green Peridot Earrings, I experimented with sanding the dot design and leaving it unsanded. In the end, I decided I liked the unsanded option better.

STRIPY CIRCLE EARRINGS

You can treat fabric the same way as paper. Coat first with sealer: the sealer will stiffen the fabric, making it easier to cut or punch. For these projects, I'm using cotton fabric, which held its colour and vibrancy beautifully. If you want to use other types of fabric, be sure to do a patch test to see if the fabric will discolour.

Materials:

- Striped fabric
- Sealer
- Stick glue
- 2 round copper 2cm (¾in) diameter bezels with loops (inner dimensions)
- 2 8mm (⁵⁄₁₆in) copper jump rings
- 2 ear wires with copper ball

Tools:

- 2cm (¾in) circle punch
- Chain-nose pliers

1 Stiffen the fabric by coating it first with sealer. Allow to dry, then punch two circles.

2 Glue one circle inside each bezel. Place the bezels on a raised, flat surface with the loops hanging over the edge. Mix the resin, pour into the bezels and allow to cure.

3 Use the pliers to open a jump ring. Slip on the bezel and an ear wire. Close the jump ring. Repeat for the second earring.

Alternative project

Multi-coloured fabric with a cheerful circle pattern offers lots of design options for this Circles Ring. Use a punch as you would with patterned paper, turning it upside down to determine which section of the design you want.

DOTTY DOMINO PENDANT

A plastic domino is the base for this fabric piece. Check out thrift stores and garage sales for spare game pieces as they can easily be repurposed into jewellery.

Materials:

- Patterned fabric
- Sealer
- 1.5 x 3cm (⅝ x 1¼in) domino piece
- Jewellery glue
- Gold pendant necklace bail
- 43cm (17in) of black rattail cord
- 2 gold spring coil ends
- Gold toggle clasp
- 2 gold 4mm (³⁄₁₆in) jump rings

Tools:

- Scissors
- Chain-nose pliers

1 Cut a piece of fabric slightly larger than the domino. Stiffen the fabric by coating it first with sealer. Allow to dry, then use sealer to glue it to the smooth side of the domino. Allow to dry.

2 Use scissors to carefully trim excess fabric around the edges of the domino.

3 Place the domino on a flat surface. Mix the resin, then use a stir stick to apply resin to the bezel. Use a cocktail stick to gently move the resin to the edges of the domino. Allow to cure.

4 Glue the bail to the back of the pendant. Slip the pendant onto the black rattail cord.

5 Glue each end of the rattail cord into a spring coil end. Allow to dry, then use the tip of the pliers to gently pinch the bottom coil end to secure.

6 Use the pliers to open one jump ring. Slip on one loop of the spring coil end. Slip on the bar half of the clasp. Close the jump ring. Repeat to attach the second spring coil end and the circular half of the clasp.

Colouring Agents

TWILIGHT GLITTER PENDANT

Because most glitter glues are water-based, they don't often mix well with resin. Keep the colour bright and undiluted by first squeezing a layer of glitter glue into your bezel, covering the bottom (see opposite, below), then allowing it to dry before adding resin on top.

Materials:

- Blue glitter glue
- Silver circle 1.6cm (⅝in) diameter pendant with loop (inner dimensions)
- 44cm (17¼in) of 3mm (⅛in) silver ball chain plus connector

1 Place the bezel on a raised, flat surface with the loop hanging over the edge. Squeeze in a layer of glitter glue. Allow to dry.

2 Mix the resin, then pour into the bezel and allow to cure.

3 Add the connector to one end of the ball chain. Slip on the pendant.

Alternative project

The Green Glitter Earrings (above) are small and sparkly – little studs add instant impact to any outfit and look great contrasted with a neutral top.

GLAM PINK GLITTER EARRINGS

These bright, vibrant earrings add sparkle and shine to any occasion. Wear with short or upswept hair for maximum impact!

Materials:

- 2 round silver 2cm (¾in) diameter bezels with loops (inner dimensions)
- Pink glitter glue
- 2 5mm (³⁄₁₆in) silver jump rings
- 2 silver ear wires

Tools:

- Chain-nose pliers

1 Place the bezels on a raised, flat surface with the loops hanging over the edge. Squeeze in a layer of glitter glue. Allow to dry.

2 Mix the resin, then pour into the bezels and allow to cure.

3 Use the pliers to open a jump ring and slip on the cured bezel and the ear wire. Close the jump ring. Repeat for the second earring.

Squeeze glitter glue into the bezel before adding resin.

WILD PLUM
HEART BRACELET

Alcohol ink colours the resin, yet it remains translucent. The metal colour of your bezel will impact the final look: a dark copper bezel filled with dark alcohol ink resin will look very dark. However, a silver bezel paired with dark alcohol ink resin will look brighter since the silver will shine through the resin.

Materials:
- Silver 1.5 x 1.8cm (⁹⁄₁₆ x ¾) heart pendant (inner dimensions), 3mm (⅛in) in depth
- Plum-coloured alcohol ink
- 20cm (7⅞in) silver charm bracelet with lobster clasp
- 5mm (³⁄₁₆in) silver jump ring

Tools:
- Chain-nose pliers

1 Place the bezel on a flat surface.

2 Mix the resin, then add a few drops of alcohol ink. Mix well, then pour into the bezel. Allow to cure.

3 Find the centre of the bracelet chain. Use the pliers to open the jump ring. Slip on the heart pendant, then slip on the centre link of the bracelet. Close the jump ring.

HAZELNUT & GOLD EARRINGS

Alcohol ink is meant to colour non-porous materials. If you mix the embossing powder into the alcohol ink/resin mixture, the alcohol ink will simply colour the powder hazelnut brown! Because the embossing powder is sprinkled on top of the earrings, it maintains its colour and adds texture you can touch.

Materials:

- 2 silver 1cm (½in) diameter round post earrings (inner dimensions)
- Hazelnut brown alcohol ink
- Gold embossing powder
- 2 earring backs

Materials:

- Packing foam

1 Insert the earrings into a foam base.

2 Mix the resin, then add a few drops of alcohol ink. Mix well, then pour into the bezel.

3 Sprinkle the top with gold embossing powder. Use a cocktail stick to guide the granules evenly. Allow to cure.

Alternative project

Because the inside of this Mountain Rose Ring is dark metal, you can brighten the effect of the alcohol ink if you place a piece of white paper or card inside the bezel first. You do need to coat the paper before adding resin, as discoloration can still show through the translucent ink.

GOLDENROD EARRINGS

Nail polish and resin can mix to create fabulous jewellery pieces. It's also a great way to use up that novelty colour of nail polish you bought on a whim! When making just one jewellery piece with one colour of nail polish, pour the amount of resin you need for your piece into a separate cup, then add the nail polish.

Materials:

> 2 antique gold large open-frame hexagon earrings, 2.5 x 2.5cm (1 x 1in) (inner dimensions)
> Yellow nail polish
> 4 small 5mm (³⁄₁₆in) antique gold jump rings
> 2 gold ear wires

Tools:

> Clear packing tape
> Chain-nose pliers

1 Place each open-frame earring on the sticky side of a small piece of clear packing tape. Press firmly to ensure the tape sticks on all edges of each earring.

2 Mix the resin, then add a few drops of nail polish. Mix well, then pour into the bezels and allow to cure. Remove the packing tape.

3 Using the pliers, open one jump ring and slip on the loop of the earring. Add a second jump ring. Close the first jump ring, then open the second jump ring and slip on the ear wire. Repeat for the second earring.

Alternative project

Bright nail polish colours mean you only need a drop or two to create vivid pieces such as these bold post Perfectly Pink Earrings.

PEACHY KEEN PENDANT

To achieve a variegated effect such as this one, I used more nail polish with the resin so the colour is bolder. However, this can affect the way the resin cures, so I created the bezel in two sessions: first, to pour the nail polish/resin mixture, then later to dome the pendant with clear resin. This ensures the piece will cure properly and gives beautiful dimension.

Materials:

- Small silver 1.5cm (⅝in) diameter pendant with loop (inner dimensions)
- Peach nail polish
- 60cm (23½in) of 1mm (¹⁄₁₆in) silver ball chain plus connector

1 Place the bezel on a raised, flat surface with the loop hanging over the edge. Mix the resin, then add several drops of nail polish. Pour into the bezel only to the rim. Use a cocktail stick to gently swirl the mixture. Allow to cure.

2 Mix some clear resin, then use a cocktail stick to apply it to the top of the cured bezel. Start at the centre, then gently spread the resin to the edges of the bezel. Allow to cure.

3 Add the connector to one end of the ball chain. Slip on the pendant.

Alternative project

These Golden Glow Earrings use the same nail polish colour as the Peachy Keen Pendant – but here I only added a little bit of nail polish to my resin, so the silver bezel shines through the translucent mixture.

BLUE & GREEN BANGLES

A few drops of paint to your resin gives you custom colour and style. I like using acrylic paint because it's widely available, comes in lots of fabulous colours and it's inexpensive. You only need a few drops of paint mixed with the resin. It doesn't take much to make the mixture thick and very opaque.

Materials:
- 2 bangles with bezels, one copper and one silver
- Blue and green acrylic paint

Tools:
- 2 kitchen sponges
- Packing foam

1 Roll a kitchen sponge and fit it inside each bangle. Cut slits in a foam base to fit each bangle, then insert the bangles with one bezel at the top.

2 Mix the resin and add a few drops of blue acrylic paint. Use a cocktail stick to fill one bezel with the resin mixture. Repeat with green paint to fill one bezel on the second bangle.

3 Let the resin set overnight, then repeat the process for the rest of the bezels.

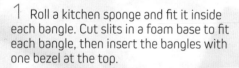

Adding resin to the bangle bezel.

Alternative project
These Simple & Stylish Painted Post Earrings are quick and easy to make. Even better, they're completely customisable. Experiment with different paint colours, ranging from brights to neon to earth tones and you'll soon have a pair for every occasion.

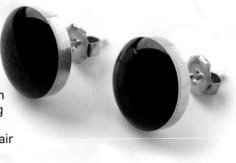

XOXO PURPLE PENDANT

A paint and resin pendant can be the focus of your jewellery piece, or a backdrop to a personalised charm. This charm was hand-stamped, but you could also use a plain charm.

Materials:
- Purple acrylic paint
- Antique copper 3 x 2cm (1¼ x ¾in) rectangular bezel with loop (inner dimensions)
- Gold metal heart charm with loop
- 3 large 8mm (⁵⁄₁₆in) gold jump rings
- Approx. 43cm (17in) of gold chain
- Gold toggle clasp
- 1 8mm (⁵⁄₁₆in) copper jump ring
- 1 small 4.5mm (³⁄₁₆in) gold jump ring

Tools:
- Metal stamping block
- Masking, washi or painter's tape
- Metal stamp letters (xoxo)
- Hammer
- Chain-nose pliers

1 Mix the resin and add a few drops of purple acrylic paint. Mix well. Pour into the bezel. Allow to cure.

2 Place the heart charm on the metal stamping block and secure with tape. Hold the 'x' metal stamp in place and strike with the hammer. Repeat to stamp 'xoxo'.

3 Use the pliers to open one large gold jump ring. Slip on one end of the chain and the circular half of the toggle clasp. Close the jump ring. Repeat to attach the bar half of the toggle clasp to the other end of the chain with a second large gold jump ring.

4 Find the centre of the chain. Use the pliers to open the copper jump ring. Slip on the centre link of the chain. Close the jump ring.

5 Use the pliers to open the third large gold jump ring. Slip on the copper jump ring and the painted pendant. Close the jump ring.

6 Use the pliers to open the small gold jump ring. Slip on the heart charm and the loop of the painted pendant. Close the jump ring.

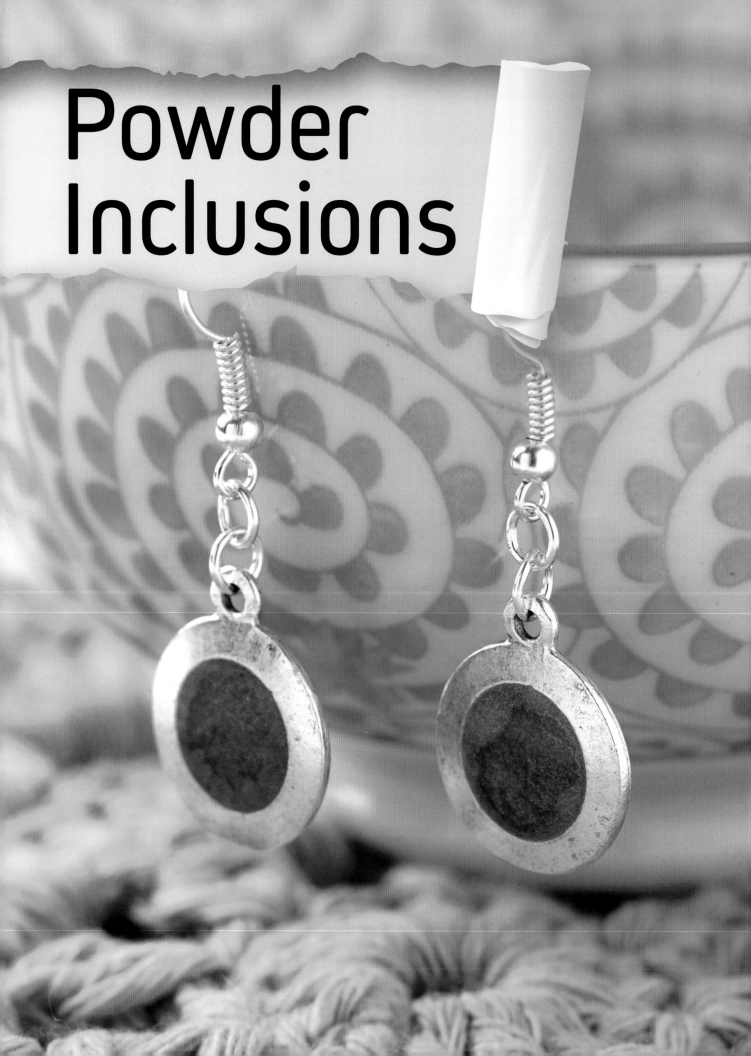

Powder
Inclusions

SILVER & GREEN PEARL NECKLACE

Enamelling powder mixed with clear resin gives a rich, dimensional addition to this decorative square bezel. I used Relique Powder. Pair it with smooth freshwater pearls and silver spacers for an elegant necklace.

Materials:

- Square silver 2cm (¾in) bezel with circular cut-out
- Chartreuse enamelling powder
- 3 silver textured 5mm (³⁄₁₆in) jump rings
- 2 silver crimp beads
- 40cm (15¾in) of fine beading wire
- Silver toggle clasp
- 4 silver textured 9mm (³⁄₈in) long beads
- 28 green oval pearls
- 28 silver daisy spacers

Tools:

- Clear packing tape
- Chain-nose pliers
- Crimping pliers

1 Place the open area of the bezel on a small piece of clear packing tape. Press firmly to ensure the tape sticks. Place the bezel on a flat surface.

2 Mix the resin, then add a small amount of chartreuse enamelling powder. Use a cocktail stick to scoop the mixture into the bezel. Allow to cure. Remove the packing tape.

3 Use the chain-nose pliers to open a textured jump ring. Slip on the pendant. Close the jump ring.

4 String a crimp bead onto the beading wire. Thread the wire through the loop of the toggle clasp. Pass the beading wire back through the crimp. Pull the beading wire so the crimp rests against the loop, leaving approximately 2cm (¾in) of beading wire on the end. Use the crimping tool to flatten the crimp.

5 String the following onto the beading wire, threading over the excess beading wire: two silver textured beads and one daisy spacer. String one pearl and one daisy spacer, then repeat to string an additional 12 pearls. String another pearl, then the pendant.

6 Reverse the bead pattern for the other half of the necklace, wrapping the wire loop around the other half of the toggle clasp and passing it back through the two silver beads before trimming excess wire.

7 Use the chain-nose pliers to open a textured jump ring. Slip it on the bottom loop of the bezel. Close the jump ring. Open a second jump ring and slip on the first jump ring, then close.

RASPBERRY & GOLD EARRINGS

A mixture of enamelling powder and resin can become opaque, even in an open-back bezel. Stir in less of the powder if you want to keep a more translucent effect.

Materials:
- 2 round 1cm (³⁄₈in) diameter open-back frames with loop (inner dimensions)
- Clear packing tape
- Raspberry enamelling powder
- 4 4.5mm (³⁄₁₆in) gold jump rings
- 2 gold ear wires

Tools:
- Chain-nose pliers

1 Place both open-back frames on a small piece of clear packing tape. Press firmly to ensure the tape sticks on all edges of each circle.

2 Mix the resin, then add a small amount of raspberry enamelling powder. Stir well.

3 Use a cocktail stick to fill the frames with the resin mixture. Allow to cure. Remove the packing tape.

4 Use the pliers to open a jump ring and slip on the cured bezel and a second jump ring. Close the first jump ring. Open the second jump ring and slip on an ear wire. Close. Repeat for the second earring.

Alternative project
Copper powder mixed with resin adds a dramatic, shimmering tone-on-tone effect when poured into a copper bezel, as in this Copper Glitz Necklace.

PERFECT GOLD EARRINGS

Pigment powders are very fine coloured powders with a built-in binder. They're often used for papercrafting techniques, but they can also be mixed with resin to provide rich colour and a bit of sparkle. Use a small spoon to scoop a bit into your resin, then mix well with a cocktail stick. I used Perfect Pearls™ for these projects.

Materials:

> 2 round 1.5cm (⅝in) diameter open-back silver drops with loops (you can use the circular half of a toggle clasp); inner dimensions 1cm (⅜in)

> Gold pigment powder

> 2 small 4.5mm (³⁄₁₆in) silver jump rings

> 2 silver ear wires

Tools:

> Clear packing tape

> Chain-nose pliers

1 Place each open-back drop on a small piece of clear packing tape. Press firmly to ensure the tape sticks on all edges of each piece.

2 Mix the resin, then add a small amount of pigment powder. Mix well, then use a cocktail stick to apply the mixture into the centre of each piece. Allow to cure. Remove the packing tape.

3 Using the pliers, open one jump ring and slip it on the loop of the drop. Slip on the ear wire. Close the jump ring. Repeat for the second earring.

WINTER WHITE NECKLACE

The pearly white colour of the pigment powder makes a simple and striking focal point. I added pearls and crystals for a special-occasion necklace, but the pendant looks fabulous on a simple chain or ball chain for a more casual look.

Materials:

- Round silver 2cm (¾in) diameter bezel with loop (inner dimensions)
- White pigment powder
- Approx. 50cm (19¾in) of fine silver beading wire
- Silver toggle clasp
- 2 silver crimp beads
- 20 clear crystal oval faceted beads, approx. 6 x 8mm (¼ x ⁵⁄₁₆in)
- 16 silver 2mm (¹⁄₁₆in) tube beads
- 24 9mm (⅜in) white oval pearls
- 4mm (³⁄₁₆in) silver jump ring
- Approx. 1cm (⅜in) of fine silver chain

Tools:

- Crimping pliers
- Chain-nose pliers

1 Place the bezel on a raised, flat surface with the loop hanging over the edge.

2 Mix the resin, then add a small amount of pigment powder. Pour into the bezel. Allow to cure.

3 String a crimp bead onto the beading wire. Thread the wire through the loop of the toggle clasp. Pass the beading wire back through the crimp. Pull the beading wire so the crimp rests against the loop, leaving approximately 2cm (¾in) of beading wire on the end. Use the crimping tool to flatten the crimp.

4 String the following onto the beading wire, threading over the excess beading wire: two crystal beads, one silver tube bead, then three pearls.

5 Repeat the sequence three more times, then string on a silver tube bead and two crystals.

6 Use the chain-nose pliers to open the jump ring. Slip on the pendant, then the chain. Close the jump ring. Slip the loop of the chain onto the thread.

7 Reverse the bead pattern for the other half of the necklace, wrapping the wire loop around the other half of the toggle clasp and passing it back through the two crystal beads before trimming excess wire.

FRENCH TEXT GLITTER RING

Clear fine glitter is inexpensive and easy to find. Mix it with the resin before you pour or simply have it on hand to sprinkle on top of wet resin. It adds sparkle without obscuring the paper or elements you might have in your bezel, and can disguise stubborn air bubbles.

Materials:

- French text paper
- White acrylic paint
- Stick glue
- Silver 13mm (½in) diameter adjustable ring with ornate circle bezel (inner dimensions), 3mm (⅛in) in depth
- Clear fine glitter

Tools:

- Paintbrush
- 12mm (½in) circle punch

1 Paint the text paper with a light coat of white paint, allowing some of the text to show through. Punch into a circle and glue inside the ring bezel.

2 Insert the ring into a foam base. Make sure the bezel is level.

3 Mix the resin, then pour into the bezel. Sprinkle with a small amount of clear fine glitter and allow to cure.

GLITTER & GLOW EARRINGS

Mix clear fine glitter with clear resin and pour for instant wear-anywhere earrings!

Materials:

- 2 round silver 12mm (½in) diameter post earrings (inner dimensions)
- 2 earring backs
- Clear fine glitter

Tools:

- Packing foam

1 Insert the post earrings into a foam base.

2 Mix the resin, then add a small amount of clear fine glitter. Stir well, pour into the bezels and allow to cure.

Adding clear fine glitter to resin.

Alternative project

I used a watch-case bezel for this Map Ring. As the bezel wasn't round, I first punched a circle of paper that was close to the correct size, then trimmed the edges to make it fit.

SALMON PINK HEART BRACELET

German glitter glass is a cousin to clear fine glitter. It's real glass shards that can be mixed with resin to add dimension to jewellery. Start with enough resin in your cup to fill your bezel, then use a small scoop to add glitter glass. The glass is fairly chunky, so start with a little and add more as needed. Keep a cocktail stick on hand after you pour it into the bezel in order to position the particles as desired.

Materials:

- Heart-shaped 1.8cm x 1.2 cm (¾ x ½in) open-back bezel (inner dimensions)
- German glitter glass in salmon pink
- 2 small 5mm (³⁄₁₆in) silver jump rings
- Approx. 16cm (6¼in) of silver chain
- Silver lobster claw clasp
- Large 8mm (⁵⁄₁₆in) silver jump ring

Tools:

- Clear packing tape
- Chain-nose pliers

1 Place the open area of the pendant on a small piece of clear packing tape. Press firmly to ensure the tape sticks firmly.

2 Mix the resin, then add a small amount of glitter glass. Mix well, then pour into the bezel and allow to cure. Remove the packing tape.

3 Using the pliers, open one small jump ring and slip it on one end of the chain. Close the jump ring.

4 Open the second small jump ring. Slip on the clasp and the other end of the chain. Close the jump ring.

5 Find the centre of the bracelet chain. Use the pliers to open the large jump ring. Slip on the pendant and the centre link of the bracelet chain. Close the jump ring.

GREEN GLITTER RING

The silver base of the ring will shine through the resin – mix in a little glitter glass to allow more silver to show, or a lot of glitter glass for more colour.

Materials:
- Sterling silver adjustable ring with 1.6cm (⅝in) pad
- German glitter glass in chartreuse

Tools:
- Packing foam

1 Insert the adjustable ring into a foam base.

2 Mix the resin, then add a small amount of German glitter glass. Use a stir stick to apply resin to the flat pad. Start from the centre and then use a cocktail stick to guide the resin out towards the edges. Allow to cure.

Alternative project
The name says it all – these Easiest Earrings Ever are quite literally the easiest I've ever made. Since the bezels are already on ear wires, all you need to do is add clear glitter glass to the resin and apply it to the bezels.

SUPER SIMPLE PINK PINS

You can use embossing powder with an embossing inkpad, as we've seen in previous pages – and you can mix your embossing powder into your resin as an inclusion. Embossing powders are available in the stamping section of your local craft store; they come in a variety of colours and textures. I usually opt for standard or fine embossing powder as it mixes well with resin. You can also choose 'distress' embossing powders or powders with chunkier granules, which will give a different effect when mixed with resin.

Materials:

- 2 antique-style brass-plated bobby pins with a 1cm (⅜in) round pad
- Magenta embossing powder

Tools:

- Packing foam

1 Insert the bobby pins horizontally into a foam base.

2 Mix the resin, then add embossing powder. Mix thoroughly. Use a cocktail stick to apply resin to the pads of the pins. Start from the centre of the flat pad and gently work out to the edges. Allow to cure.

FAUX ONYX RING

Classic black embossing powder gives texture and shine to this simple gold ring blank.

Materials:
- Antique gold adjustable ring with 13mm (½in) diameter pad
- Black embossing powder

Tools:
- Packing foam

77

1 Insert the ring into a foam base.

2 Mix the resin, then add embossing powder and mix again. Use a cocktail stick to apply resin to the flat pad of the ring. Start from the centre and gently work out to the edges. Allow to cure.

Alternative project

These vibrant, stylish Classic Red Earrings have a timeless appeal. The embossing powder gives depth to the resin and the colour contrasts with the bright silver post bezels. They are quick and easy to make.

3-D
Inclusions

MIXED METAL & PEARL NECKLACE

With resin, a little metal gilding flake goes a long way. Use a cocktail stick to spoon the mixture into your bezel, then use it to move the flake around until you're happy with the colour combination.

Materials:

- Antique copper 2.5 x 1cm (1 x ⅜in) rectangle bezel with double loop (inner dimensions), with a depth of 1.5mm (¹⁄₁₆in)
- Metal gilding flake (I used Mega-Flake)
- 2 small 5mm (³⁄₁₆in) copper jump rings
- Antique copper toggle clasp
- 2 lengths of antique copper chain, each 13cm (5in) long
- 2 copper crimp beads
- 2 lengths of fine beading wire, each 15cm (6in) long
- 2 8mm (⁵⁄₁₆in) carved bronze metal beads
- 4 bronze-coloured 8mm (⁵⁄₁₆in) rondelle glass beads
- 4 7mm (¼in) carved silver beads
- 2 large 9mm (⅜in) gold off-round freshwater pearls
- 2 light blue ringed 1cm (⅜in) freshwater pearls
- 2 small 5mm (³⁄₁₆in) gold jump rings
- 2 copper rice freshwater pearls, 6mm (¼in) long
- Antique copper 1.5 x 1cm (⅝ x ⅜in) fleur-de-lis charm
- 2 small 5mm (³⁄₁₆in) gold off-round freshwater pearls

Tools:

- Chain-nose pliers
- Crimping pliers

1 Place the bezel on a raised, flat surface.

2 Mix the resin, then add some metal gilding flake. Use a stir stick to scoop the mixture into the bezel. Use a cocktail stick to move the flakes around in the mixture until you're happy with the arrangement. Allow to cure.

3 Use the chain-nose pliers to open one small copper jump ring. Slip on the circular half of the toggle clasp and one end of one piece of chain. Close the jump ring. Repeat with the bar half of the clasp and the second piece of chain.

4 String a crimp bead onto one piece of beading wire. Loop the wire around the end of one piece of chain. Pass the beading wire back through the crimp. Pull the beading wire so the crimp rests against the chain, leaving approximately 2cm (¾in) of beading wire on the end. Use the crimping pliers to flatten the crimp.

5 String the following onto the beading wire, threading over the excess beading wire: one carved bronze metal bead, one glass rondelle, one carved silver metal bead, one large gold pearl, one glass rondelle, one light blue pearl, one small gold pearl, one carved silver metal bead, one copper rice pearl.

6 Use the pliers to open one small gold jump ring. Slip on the pendant, then string the pendant on the beading wire.

7 Reverse the bead pattern for the other half of the necklace, wrapping the wire loop around the last link in the second piece of chain and passing it back through at least three beads before trimming excess wire.

8 Use the chain-nose pliers to open the second gold jump ring. Slip on the fleur-de-lis charm and the bottom loop of the pendant. Close the jump ring.

ROYAL PEACOCK PENDANT

The varied colours of the metal flake gives you limitless possibilities for capturing different shades of metallic copper, gold or teal.

Materials:

- Round 1.6cm (⅝in) silver pendant with loop (inner dimensions)
- Metal gilding flake
- 40cm (15¾in) of 3mm (⅛in) silver ball chain plus connector

1 Place the bezel on a raised, flat surface with the loop hanging over the edge.

2 Mix the resin, then add metal flake inclusions. Use the stir stick to scoop the mixture into the bezel. Use the cocktail stick to move the flakes around in the mixture until you're happy with the arrangement. Allow to cure.

3 Add the connector to one end of the ball chain. Slip on the pendant.

Alternative project

For this Steampunk Watch Case Pendant, a big open-back watch case was the perfect place for variegated metal gilding flake and watch parts.

SHINE BROOCH

You can create this brooch in one resin session. However, if you want to create layers of 'floating' glitter glass, create the bezel in two sessions. Simply fill the bezel halfway with resin and allow to cure, then sprinkle more glitter glass onto the cured surface and add more resin. This will give a dimensional effect. When adding watch parts, keep an eye out for air bubbles. If necessary, use a toothpick to pierce any bubbles that might occur around the inclusions.

Materials:
- Blue/cream patterned paper
- Sealer
- Stick glue
- Computer-generated word or word cut from text paper
- Round silver 3.2cm (1¼in) diameter brooch with ornate border (inner dimensions)
- Watch parts
- German glitter glass in gold

Tools:
- 3cm (1¼in) circle punch
- Packing foam

1 Punch a circle from patterned paper. Coat with sealer, then allow to dry and glue inside the bezel.

2 Glue the word to the patterned paper. Insert the brooch into a foam base. Arrange the watch parts as desired and sprinkle in glitter glass, using a cocktail stick to move elements.

3 Mix the resin, then use a stir stick to apply resin to the bezel. Use a cocktail stick to guide some of the glitter fragments evenly in the bezel. Allow to cure.

Alternative project
Which crafter doesn't have a jar of spare buttons? I confess to having several – and I love shopping for vintage buttons at flea markets. As you can see with this fun Button Hairclip, they don't even have to match!

DRAGONFLY BRACELET

Watch parts come in many different metal finishes, so it's fun to carry the theme through the rest of your jewellery piece, with mixed-metal chain, charm and bezel.

Materials:

> Book paper
> White acrylic paint
> Stick glue
> 1.5cm (⅝in) square antique copper pendant with loop (inner dimensions)
> Watch parts
> 4 5mm (³⁄₁₆in) gold jump rings
> 17cm (6¾in) of antique copper chain
> 17cm (6¾in) of gold chain
> Gold toggle clasp
> Gold dragonfly charm

Tools:

> Paintbrush
> 1.5cm (⅝in) square punch
> Chain-nose pliers

1 Paint the book paper white. Allow to dry, then punch a square. Glue inside the bezel. Allow to dry.

2 Place the bezel on a flat surface with the loop hanging off the edge. Arrange the watch parts as desired, using a cocktail stick to move elements.

3 Mix the resin, then use the stir stick to apply resin to the bezel. Use the cocktail stick to guide some of the watch part pieces evenly in the bezel. Allow to cure.

4 Use the pliers to open a jump ring. Slip on one end of each piece of chain, and the circular half of the toggle clasp. Close the jump ring. Repeat for the other end of the chain and the bar half of the clasp.

5 Find the centre of the two pieces of chain. Use the pliers to open the third jump ring. Slip on the bezel and the two centre links of the chain. Close the jump ring.

6 Use the pliers to open the last jump ring. Slip on the dragonfly charm and a link on the copper chain, about four links from the pendant. Close the jump ring.

FEATHER PENDANT

Natural materials such as feathers are beautiful when preserved in an open-back pendant and sealed with resin. My daughter found this small feather on a walk and it was too pretty not to preserve. This large pendant can be worn as a necklace as shown here, or you could turn it into a brooch or handbag charm.

Materials:

- 25 x 44cm (9¾ x 17¼in) rectangular open-back bezel (inner dimensions)
- Book paper
- Feather (found or commercial)
- German glitter glass in silver
- Small and medium crystal gemstone stickers
- Silver headpin
- 1cm (³⁄₈in) blue bead
- 2 medium 6mm (¼in) silver jump rings
- 2 small 4mm (³⁄₁₆in) silver jump rings
- 52cm (20½in) of silver chain
- Silver toggle clasp

Tools:

- 5cm (2in) piece of kitchen sponge
- Clear packing tape
- Scissors
- Round-nose pliers
- Chain-nose pliers

This pendant is created in two sessions. For the first session:

1 Place the open area of the pendant on a small piece of clear packing tape. Press firmly to ensure the tape sticks firmly. Mix the resin, then pour a shallow layer inside the bezel, about halfway to the top. Allow to cure.

2 Tear a small piece of book paper (approximately 1 x 25cm (⅜ x 9¾in). Use the kitchen sponge to coat the front and back with resin. Allow to cure.

3 Place the feather on the craft sheet and use the sponge to coat the front and back with resin. Allow to cure.

4 Add silver glitter glass to the resin and stir well, then pour a small puddle onto the craft sheet. Use a stir stick to spread it into a shape approximately 3 x 3cm (1¼ x 1¼in). Allow to cure.

For the second session:

5 Place a strip of book paper inside the bezel on top of the cured layer of resin. Trim to fit, if necessary. Use scissors to cut a piece of silver glitter glass resin and place at the right side of the bezel. Add the crystal gemstone stickers. Finally, place the feather into the bezel.

6 Mix the resin, then fill the rest of the bezel. Use the cocktail stick to guide any elements that might shift. Allow to cure. Remove the packing tape.

7 Insert the headpin in the bead. Use the round-nose pliers to form a loop; use the chain-nose pliers to form a wire wrapped loop. Use the chain-nose pliers to open a medium jump ring. Slip on the loop of the bead and the bottom loop of the bezel.

8 Use chain-nose pliers to open the loop of one small jump ring. Slip on one end of the chain and the circular half of the clasp. Repeat to connect the bar half of the clasp and the other end of the chain.

9 Find the centre of the chain. Use the chain-nose pliers to open the second medium jump ring. Slip on the top loop of the bezel and the centre loop of the chain.

Alternative projects

Below: A trip to the beach is the perfect opportunity to collect treasures such as small shells. Preserve them in a pretty pendant that becomes a keepsake jewellery piece, as in this By The Sea Pendant.

Below right: Flattened leaves and flowers work best as inclusions, especially in shallow bezels. You can flatten materials with a flower press or between the pages of a heavy book, as I did with this Reverie Leaf Pendant.

No-bezel Jewellery

HEART TRIO BRACELET

Your resin mixture doesn't have to fit only inside a bezel – you can also add it on top of another surface, such as a wooden shape. Take care not to allow the resin to spill over the shape: unlike a bezel, there are no edges to hold it in!

Materials:

- 3 wooden hearts, 2.5cm (1in) at widest point
- Stick glue
- Sheet music
- Acrylic paint in red and teal
- Jewellery glue
- 3 silver pendant bails
- Large silver 8mm (⁵⁄₁₆in) jump ring
- Approx. 19cm (7½in) of silver chain
- Silver lobster claw clasp
- 4 small 5mm (³⁄₁₆in) silver jump rings

Tools:

- Scissors
- Emery board
- Paintbrush
- Stipple brush or old toothbrush
- Clear acrylic block
- Butterfly stamp
- Black dye-based inkpad
- Chain-nose pliers

1 For the musical heart, glue sheet music paper onto a heart and use scissors to trim around the outside edges. Sand the edges with the emery board if necessary.

2 For the teal and red heart, paint one heart with teal paint. Allow to dry. Make a watery wash of red paint and use the stipple brush to spatter onto the heart. Allow to dry.

3 For the stamped heart, ink the butterfly stamp with black, then press onto the heart.

4 Place all three hearts on a craft sheet. Mix the resin, then use a cocktail stick to apply the resin to the hearts. Start in the centre and guide the resin to the edges with the cocktail stick. Allow to cure on a craft sheet. That way, you can simply lift off the piece even if the resin does overflow a bit and cause the heart to adhere to the craft sheet.

5 Glue a pendant bail to the back of each heart using jewellery glue. Use the pliers to attach the large jump ring on one end of the chain. Attach one small jump ring and the lobster clasp to the other end.

6 Find the centre of the bracelet chain. Use the pliers to open a small jump ring. Slip on the teal heart and the centre loop of the chain. Close the jump ring. Repeat to attach the other two hearts about 2.5cm (1in) on either side of the centre heart.

GLITTER HEART HAIRPIN

Mixing glitter into the resin will make a thicker substance that is slightly less apt to overflow the flat wooden piece. However, take care to start the resin in the centre of the wooden piece and use the cocktail stick to guide it outwards.

Materials:

- Wooden heart, 2.5cm (1in) at widest point
- Red acrylic paint
- Clear fine glitter
- Jewellery glue
- Silver bobby pin with a 1cm (⅜in) round pad

Tools:

- Paintbrush

1 Paint the heart red. Allow to dry, then place it on a craft sheet.

2 Mix the resin, then add clear glitter. Use the stir stick to apply resin to the centre of the heart shape. Use the cocktail stick to gently guide the resin to the edges of the shape. Allow to cure.

3 Glue the heart shape to the flat pad of the pin and allow to dry.

Guiding resin into place with a cocktail stick.

ORIGAMI PENDANT

I added silver stickers in the flower centres of this design. You can choose dimensional rhinestone stickers as I did here – these will not be entirely covered by the resin – or you can opt for flat, metallic stickers.

Materials:

- Flowery origami paper
- Sealer
- Rectangular wooden game piece
- 2 round silver rhinestone stickers
- Jewellery glue
- Silver pendant necklace bail
- 3 small 5mm (³/₁₆in) silver jump rings
- 44cm (17¼in) of silver chain
- Silver toggle clasp

Tools:

- Emery board
- Safety mask
- Chain-nose pliers

1 Cut a small piece of origami paper slightly larger than the game piece. Coat with sealer and allow to dry.

2 Apply sealer to the flat side of the wooden game piece. Place the origami paper on top and smooth. Trim excess paper from the edges of the game piece. Coat the top and edges of the paper with sealer.

3 Allow to dry, then add a rhinestone sticker at the centre of each flower. Use the emery board to sand along the edges of the wooden rectangle to create completely smooth sides. Wear a safety mask while sanding.

4 Place the wooden piece on a craft sheet. Mix the resin, then use the stir stick to apply resin to the wooden piece.

Begin at the centre, then work the resin to the edges of the rectangle with the cocktail stick. Allow to cure.

5 Glue the bail to the back of the wooden game piece.

6 Use the pliers to open a jump ring. Slip on one end of the chain and the loop of the circular half of the toggle clasp. Close the jump ring. Repeat to attach the bar half of the toggle clasp to the other end of the chain.

7 Find the centre of the necklace. Use the pliers to open the third jump ring. Slip on the centre loop of the chain and the pendant bail. Close the jump ring.

BERLIN SCRABBLE® TILE

Map paper, especially old map paper, is very porous and has often been handled a lot, so I used two coats of sealer to make sure of avoiding discoloration.

Materials:

- Sealer
- Square wooden game piece
- Map paper
- Jewellery glue
- Silver pendant necklace bail
- 52cm (20½in) of 1mm (¹⁄₁₆in) silver ball chain plus connector

Tools:

- 2.5cm (1in) square punch (optional) or scissors
- Emery board
- Safety mask
- Cocktail stick

1 Punch or cut a section of map paper. Coat with sealer and allow to dry.

2 Apply sealer to the flat side of the game piece. Place the map paper on top and smooth. Trim excess paper. Coat the top and edges of the paper with sealer. Use the emery board to sand along the edges of the wooden square to create completely smooth sides. Wear a safety mask while sanding.

3 Place the wooden piece on a craft sheet. Mix the resin, then use the stir stick to apply resin to the wooden piece. Begin at the centre, then work the resin to the edges of the rectangle with the cocktail stick. Allow to cure.

4 Glue the bail to the back of the wooden game piece using jewellery glue.

5 Add the connector to one end of the ball chain. Slip on the pendant.

FOREVER BLUE NECKLACE

You can use your craft sheet to create free-form resin shapes. Mix the resin and add colouring agents if you wish. You can pour the resin onto a craft sheet, or use a stir stick to drizzle the resin. Use a stir stick to manipulate the resin into a shape. If you plan to move the craft sheet before the piece is dry, place a cutting board underneath first so it stays level when you lift it.

Materials:
- Blue pigment powder
- Gold pendant necklace bail
- Jewellery glue
- 3 8mm (⁵⁄₁₆in) gold jump rings
- 44cm (17¼in) of gold chain
- Gold toggle clasp

Tools:
- Emery board
- Safety mask
- Chain-nose pliers

1 Mix the resin, then add pigment powder. Use a stir stick to place a circle-shaped puddle on your craft sheet.

2 When the resin has cured, peel the piece off the craft sheet. Use the emery board to sand the edges if necessary. Wear a safety mask while sanding.

3 Glue the bail to the back of the cured resin piece with jewellery glue.

4 Use the pliers to open one of the jump rings. Slip on one end of the chain and the loop of the circular half of the toggle clasp. Close the jump ring. Repeat to attach the bar half of the toggle clasp to the other end of the chain.

5 Find the centre of the necklace. Use the pliers to open the third jump ring. Slip on the centre loop of the chain and the pendant bail. Close the jump ring.

Alternative project
This Green Faux Stone Necklace is coloured with acrylic paint. When this is combined with resin, it can result in a somewhat rubbery or flexible piece, so you might need to do a second resin session. I coated the top and bottom with clear resin. If the flexibility doesn't bother you, leave it as it is.

GLITTER SQUARE NECKLACE

This lightweight pendant is made in two resin sessions. The first is to create a thin piece of glittery resin on the craft sheet, which can be punched. The second session is to add another layer of resin to make the pendant thicker. Repeat until the piece reaches the desired thickness.

Materials:

- German glitter glass in salmon pink
- 2 small 5mm (³/₁₆in) silver jump rings
- Approx. 40cm (15¾in) of silver chain
- Silver toggle clasp
- Large 9mm (³/₈in) silver jump ring

Tools:

- 3cm (1¼in) square punch
- 3mm (⅛in) circle hole punch
- Chain-nose pliers
- Emery board
- Safety mask

1 Mix the resin, then add German glitter glass. Stir well, then use the stir stick to place a thin layer of glittery resin on your craft sheet – about 4–5cm (1½–2in) in size. Allow to cure.

2 Peel the piece off the craft sheet. Punch into a square shape. Use the circle hole punch to make a hole at the top for the jump ring.

3 To thicken the piece, place the square on the craft sheet. Mix more resin, then pour on top of the punched square. Use the cocktail stick to guide the resin to the corners and edges, avoiding the punched hole. Allow to cure.

4 Use the pliers to open a small jump ring. Slip on the last loop of the chain and the circular half of the toggle clasp. Close the jump ring. Repeat to attach the bar half of the toggle clasp to the other end of the chain.

5 Find the centre of the necklace. Use the pliers to open the large jump ring. Slip through the punched hole of the square pendant and onto the chain. Close the jump ring.

POOL BLUE EARRINGS

Commercial resin moulds are readily available in lots of different shapes and sizes. Prepare your resin mixture and add colouring agents if desired. Place the mould on a flat surface. Pour resin into the mould, taking care not to overflow. Let it cure, then pop out the shape. You might need to sand the edges with an emery board.

Materials:
- Blue acrylic paint
- White pigment powder
- German glitter glass in silver
- 4 8mm (5/16in) silver jump rings
- 2 round 1.5cm (5/8in) silver open-back drops with loops
- Jewellery glue

Tools:
- Resin epoxy mould with rectangle shapes
- Emery board
- Safety mask
- Chain-nose pliers

1 Mix the resin, then add the blue paint. Add white pigment powder until you have a pearly blue.

2 Place the mould on a flat surface. Sprinkle silver glitter glass into two small rectangle shapes on the mould, then pour in the resin mixture. Add more silver glitter glass on top of the resin. Remember that the bottom of the mould shape will form the front of your jewellery piece.

3 Allow to cure, then flex the mould to remove the shapes. If necessary, use the emery board to sand the edges. Wear a safety mask while sanding.

4 Glue each resin rectangle to a silver drop. Use the pliers to open a jump ring. Slip on the drop and a second jump ring. Close the first jump ring and open the second. Slip on the ear wire and close the loop. Repeat for the second earring.

Alternative project
Dimensional inclusions such as stones can be preserved in resin for one-of-a-kind pieces. I bought some amber stones in a souvenir shop in Gdansk, which is famous for Baltic amber – so this Amber Necklace piece (right) is a nice memory of my time in Poland. Have fun creating jewellery with memorabilia from your holidays and travels.

NEON CIRCLE NECKLACE

Although the mould for this piece is meant for making earrings, I love layering the brightly coloured circle shapes for a fun pendant.

Materials:

> Magenta embossing powder
> Yellow embossing powder
> Jewellery glue
> Approx. 55cm(21¾in) of black rattail cord
> 2 silver cord ends
> 2 small 5mm (³⁄₁₆in) silver jump rings
> Large silver toggle clasp

Tools:

> Resin epoxy mould with circle shapes
> Emery board
> Safety mask
> Chain-nose pliers

1 Place the mould on a flat surface. Mix the resin, then add magenta embossing powder. Pour into the large earring shape of the mould.

2 Repeat to mix resin with yellow embossing powder and pour into the medium shape on the mould.

3 Allow the resin to set, then pop out the circles and sand the edges with the emery board. Wear a safety mask while sanding.

4 Glue each end of the rattail cord into a cord end using jewellery glue. Allow to dry, then use the tip of the pliers to gently fold in each side of the cord end.

5 Fold the rattail cord in half lengthwise with the loose ends even. Hold the two resin circles together. Thread the folded end of the rattail through the centres of the resin circles. Thread the loose ends of the rattail cord back through the loop and pull taut.

6 Use the pliers to open one jump ring. Slip on the loop of the circular half of the toggle clasp and one end of the rattail. Close the loop. Repeat for the bar half of the clasp.

Alternative project

This Grape Fizz Heart necklace features a toggle clasp in the front for added interest. For designs such as these, it's best to use a larger toggle to keep in proportion to the larger pendant shape. This keeps the design looking bold and contemporary.

Index